Good Sp

Written by Bob Eschenbach   **Photographs by Graham Meadows**

Today we are playing games at school.
We are playing soccer.
We are playing Mrs. Brown's class.

We have the soccer ball.
We kick off first.
We kick the ball
to the boys and girls on our team.

Our teacher shouts, "GO, TEAM, GO!"

Mrs. Brown shouts, "GO, TEAM, GO!"

Mrs. Brown's class gets the ball.
The boys and girls in Mrs. Brown's class
kick the ball to each other.
The boys and girls in Mrs. Brown's class
score a goal.

They have one goal.
We have no goals.

Our teacher shouts, "GO, TEAM, GO!"

Mrs. Brown shouts, "GO, TEAM, GO!"

We get the ball.
We kick the ball to each other.
A girl on our team scores a goal.
Mrs. Brown's class has one goal,
and we have one goal.

Mrs. Brown's class has the ball.
The boys and girls kick the ball
to each other.
They kick the ball into the goal.
Mrs. Brown's class has two goals.
We have one goal.

Mrs. Brown's class jumps up and down.
They are the winners.

We jump up and down, too.
We jump up and down for Mrs. Brown's class.

We say that they are the best players.
They say that we are the best sports.